For Talia,
and to the memory of Jack Solomon,
who made "uncle" a most wonderful word

—M. K.

To Victoria, Cecilia, and Gina—
for all your help with the fishy details,
getting them right and making them all fit nicely

—S. D. S.

I first of all owe a very large thank you to Christine Toomey and Ines, who first started me thinking about writing books for young people. I also want to thank Charlotte Sheedy, Ramona Peters for her advice on the Wampanoag people, and I most gratefully want to thank Victoria Wells and Nancy Paulsen for so skillfully putting this book together. A most special thanks to Talia Feiga Kurlansky for all you teach me, and to Marian Mass for all we share. —M. K.

For the endpapers, special thanks to my brother, Thomas Schindler, for his instruction on *gyotaku*, a Japanese fish-printing method used to record the size of a fisherman's catch. In this book the print was made with gouache on rice paper using a whole cod as a template. The rest of the art was done in watercolor and inks on watercolor paper. —S. D. S.

The Cod's Tale

by MARK KURLANSKY

illustrated by S. D. SCHINDLER

G. P. Putnam's Sons   New York

INTRODUCTION: THE BIGGEST SCHOOL

Fish almost never swim alone. That is why a fisherman who has caught one fish will quickly throw his hook or net back in the water and try to catch more. Fish swim, hunt, eat—spend their lives in groups. A group of fish is called a school. This is not because it is a place of learning. It is an old word from Holland that means a crowd. Fish live in crowds.

The largest school of fish ever known lived in the Atlantic Ocean off Canada and the northeastern part of the United States. So many fish lived in this school that they would bump into one another when swimming.

These fish were the Atlantic cod, and they were to become not only the most commonly eaten fish in the Western world, but also one of the most valuable items of trade. Valued like gold or oil, cod played a central role in the history of North America and Europe.

It was cod that enabled the Vikings to come to North America. The search for cod brought Europeans across the ocean and encouraged the Pilgrims to settle in Massachusetts. It fed African slaves and financed the slave trade, was the first frozen food, and finally, changed the modern laws of the sea.

Today, cod are no longer plentiful, and its threatened disappearance is a tragedy that could change the lives of many creatures, including man. This is the cod's story.

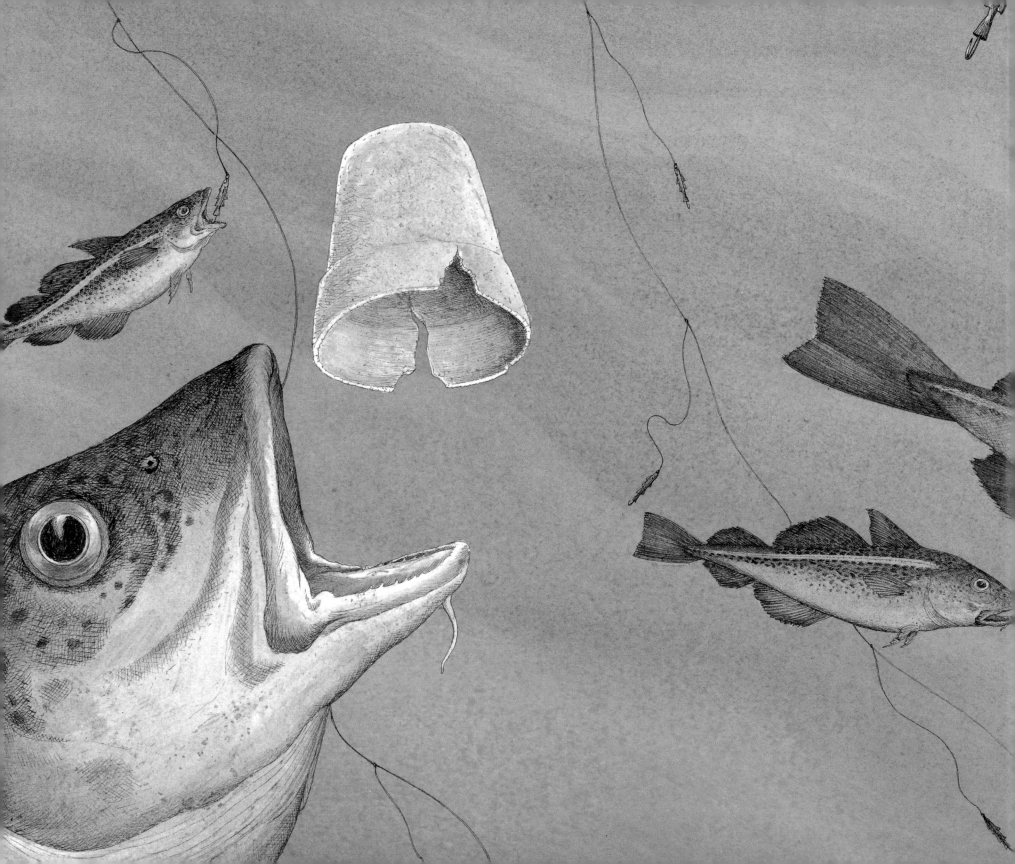

The Codfish

The Atlantic cod is a large and ugly fish. It is often more than three feet long and has gray or brown skin, yellow or gold spots on its back, and an odd whiskerlike feeler hanging from its chin.

The cod spends its life swimming with its big mouth wide open, trying to swallow whatever will fit. It will even eat small young cod. It also eats things that are far less tasty. Styrofoam coffee cups have been found in cod stomachs. Almost any bait or object, even a fish-shaped piece of lead, can attract a cod. The cod's greedy appetite makes it easy to catch.

LIFE CYCLE

A single codfish will lay millions of eggs. The larger the fish, the more eggs she produces. Fish grow larger every year of their lives. A cod that is forty inches long can produce three million eggs at once. But a cod that is fifty inches long can produce nine million eggs. The longer a cod lives, the more young cod she can produce. If a cod can avoid fishermen and other predators, it can live thirty years. By then it is as large as a man and produces many millions of eggs.

For centuries it was thought that with so many eggs, cod would always be plentiful. But now we have learned that this isn't true. Most of the eggs do not survive. In the ocean world, in which big fish eat smaller fish and smaller fish eat still smaller ones, it is very dangerous for the smallest creatures. Cod eggs are the size of a very small bead and float unprotected near the ocean's surface.

Two weeks after the eggs arrive, almost all of them have been eaten or destroyed by storms. The few surviving eggs hatch into tiny cod. They are extremely hungry and must eat constantly so that they can grow.

At first they eat phytoplankton, creatures so small that they appear not as individual animals, but as a cloud in the water. After a few days of eating, the cod are large enough to eat the slightly bigger zooplankton. Days later, still not an inch long, they are large enough to eat krill, which resemble tiny shrimp.

But there is competition for this food. Herring, mackerel, and other small fish also eat krill, and while they are at it, they eat the baby cod. The humpback whale, with its huge, open mouth, moves through the water like a factory-sized scoop.

After a few weeks the surviving cod are about an inch and a half long and translucent. They are called juveniles and are big enough to leave the dangerous surface of the ocean and dive to the bottom of the sea. There they look for rocks and other places to hide from the larger fish that hunt them.

ENEMIES

If the young cod can stay alive for the first year, they will now be big enough not to fear other fish that swim above them. The cod can swim up and eat smaller fish or dive back to the bottom and eat mussels and other shellfish. As it is one of the larger fish, few animals will eat the full-grown cod. But they still have two deadly enemies. One is the seal. Seals love to eat cod, but they do not like bones. So they bite the cod in the belly and throw the rest away. The other, more deadly enemy of the cod is man.

People will eat almost every part of the cod. Some think the head is the most flavorful part, especially the cheeks and the part under the chin that is sometimes called the tongue. People also eat the eggs, stomach, and liver.

Oil from the liver is given to children because it is rich in vitamins. Most agree the oil has a horrible taste. In Scotland, cod liver is stuffed in cod stomachs and called Crappin-Muggie, a name that sounds as unappealing as the dish itself. In Iceland, they grill cod skin and serve it with butter. And long ago, when the people in Iceland were very poor, they sometimes soaked cod bones until they were soft, and ate them too.

ON CHOOSING A FRESH COD

"The head should be large; tail small; shoulders thick; liver, creamy white; and the skin clear and silvery with a bronze-like sheen."

—Manual of Naval Cookery, British Admiralty, 1921

THE CONTINENTAL SHELF

It is easy to imagine that the ocean is full of fish. But we only think that because fish live near us—close to the land. Most fish live on continental shelves, the part of the land that extends from the shore under the ocean, in some places for only twenty miles and in others for hundreds of miles. In that shallower water, sunlight helps tiny sea organisms grow and become food for fish like cod.

Crossing the Atlantic Ocean from America to Europe, a boat sails past many fish when it first leaves America. Then, once it goes beyond the North American continental shelf, it may go for days without being near a fish. As it gets close to Europe, approaching the European shelf, fish appear again.

But in the northern part of the globe where cod live, the continents are close to each other. Britain is close to Iceland, which is close to Greenland, which is close to Labrador and Newfoundland. The shelves of these landmasses are even closer, and the water is cold. Since cod live on shelves and like cold water, this is the one place where the ocean can be crossed without ever being far from cod.

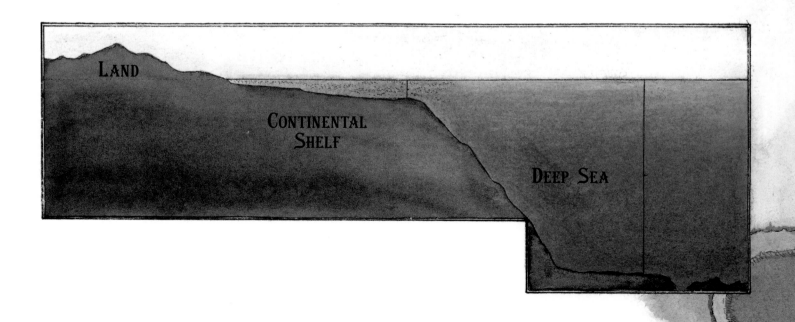

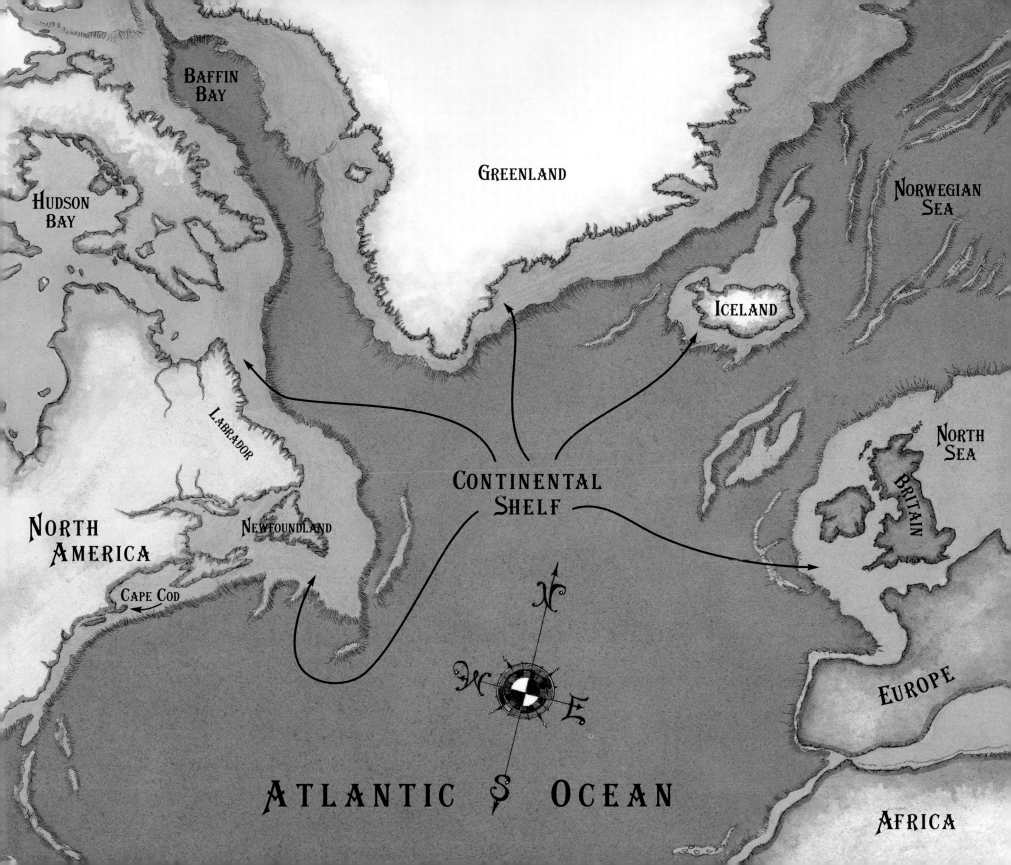

VIKINGS

Between the years 800 and 1100, the Vikings left their homes in Norway, Sweden, and Denmark to travel farther than Europeans had ever gone before—throughout Europe and all the way across the cold North Atlantic.

They were able to travel such long distances because they had solved two of the great problems of ocean travel. First, the hull, or bottom, of a Viking ship could endure months of pounding ocean waves because the Vikings overlapped the planks instead of just placing them next to each other. And secondly, they had food perfect for travel—dried cod. The Vikings learned to hang the cod in the cold, dry arctic air until it was as hard as wood. This tough, dry food had no fat, was full of protein, and would not spoil.

Prehistoric times British and Scandinavians start to fish for cod in the North Sea.

circa A.D. 600 The Basques begin hunting whales.

circa 800 The Vikings begin traveling out of Scandinavia. Basques in southern France learn shipbuilding techniques from these raiders.

circa 861 The Vikings discover Iceland.

The Vikings were traders, constantly in search of goods. Their limited northern products made from fur, reindeer antlers, and walrus tusks were not enough for a prosperous trade, so they also sold into slavery people they captured by attacking villages in Britain and France.

This made the Vikings a feared warlike tribe. No Viking was more feared than Erik the Red. His father had been expelled from his native Norway for killing people and then Erik was expelled from Iceland for the same thing. He left Iceland in about 982 with his son Leif Eriksson and a band of followers.

On a small, open-decked ship they sailed west over the dark sea. The waves sometimes rolled three times the height of the Vikings' mast and threatened to crush them. But with their sail and oars they skillfully rode on just the right side of each wave until they arrived in a land of glaciers, rocks, and icebergs that glowed robin's egg blue.

STOCKFISH

When it (cod) is taken in the far seas and it is desired to keep it for 10 or 12 years, it is gutted and its head removed and it is dried in the air and sun and in no wise by a fire, or smoked; and when this is done it is called stockfish. And when it hath been kept a long time, and it is desired to eat it, it must be beaten with a wooden hammer for a full hour, then set it to soak in warm water for a full 12 hours or more, then cook and skim it very well like beef.

—*le Mesnagier de Paris*, author unknown, circa 1393

circa 982 Erik leads the Vikings from Iceland to Greenland.

circa 1000 Leif Eriksson makes first of several trips to North America.

Erik found a new land, which he named "Greenland" to attract settlers. But there was no green—only white and blue ice and black and gray rock. The Vikings built a small colony. But after a few years, hoping to find a better place, they caught more cod and hung it from poles to dry until they had enough food to sail farther west.

Then, just as they were about to leave, Erik hurt his foot in a horse-riding accident. He had to stay in Greenland, so his son Leif Eriksson led the next journey. Leif sailed on to a place he called "Stoneland," which was probably the rocky Labrador coast of Canada, and then to "Woodland" and "Vineland."

The identity of these places is not certain.
They may have been Newfoundland, Nova Scotia,
or Maine. The Vikings found little food in these places,
and angry tribesmen often attacked them. But they could
keep traveling because they had their hard, dried fish to break
off and eat like stale bread during long winter months.

Many historians did not believe that the Vikings had been to North
America, until 1960, when the remains of eight Viking-built turf houses
dating from the year 1000 were found in Newfoundland, proving that they had
been to America long before Christopher Columbus.

THE VIRTUES OF WOOD

(Stockfish is) hard as lumps of wood, but free of bad flavor, in fact, without much flavor at all . . . though very nice as an appetizer, and after all, anything that performs that function cannot be all that bad.

—Poggio Bracciolini, 1436 (celebrated Latin scholar)

THE BIG SECRET

The Basques were probably the next Europeans to visit America. In the fourteenth and fifteenth centuries most European fishing communities had heard rumors that the Basques were fishing in a land across the sea.

The Basques live in a small area of velvety green mountains with rocky crests that is partly in southwestern France and partly in Spain. But they are neither Spanish nor French. They have their own customs, traditions, and language.

The Basques were the first people to hunt whales for profit. At first they caught them near their beaches. But in the ninth century, the Vikings came to the land of the Basques. The Basques were able to discover how to build ships that could travel long distances the way the Vikings' had. With these new strong ships the Basques chased whales into northern waters, covering the sound of their oars with cloth so they could row up to the sleeping black giants and plunge their long harpoons into the whales' sides.

THE CHASSE D'EAU

To prepare salt cod it must be soaked in water for twenty-four hours or longer. Ideally, the water should be changed from time to time. In 1947, the president of the Conseil, the governing body of France, asked his valet to flush the toilet once an hour for the next week in preparation for a special dinner he was preparing on Sunday. The dish was dried cod. The toilet was fed by a water tank mounted high up on the wall, the *chasse d'eau*. A stockfish left in the *chasse d'eau* for two days was soft and ready for cooking.

The Basques traveled far north for whales, and by about 1400, they found the crowded school of cod on the coast of North America where the Vikings had fished.

By 1400 many of the Vikings had become Christian and had settled in various parts of northern Europe. The colonists on Greenland had died off, and the Basques had the waters of North America to themselves. They began to sell cod in Europe, the first to earn money from North American fish.

Because the Basques were growing very rich selling cod, they did not want to tell anyone where they had found this huge school of fish. They did not claim the land. They built no settlements, though they did have camps in the summer where whale fat was cooked into oil and where the codfish were spread open, salted, and dried. Then, in the fall, they loaded their ships with barrels of whale oil and dried fish that they took back to Europe to sell.

Refrigeration and freezing had not yet been invented, and fresh fish spoiled quickly, so only people who lived on the coast could eat fish. But the salted cod of the Basques could be stacked in carts and carried inland without spoiling. For the first time many Europeans could eat fish.

SALTING

The Basques did not just dry the cod as the Vikings had, they salted it too. Unlike the Vikings the Basques had a plentiful salt supply from trade in the Mediterranean. Dried and salted cod preserved even better, and it could be soaked in water and turned back into a soft, flaky fish.

23

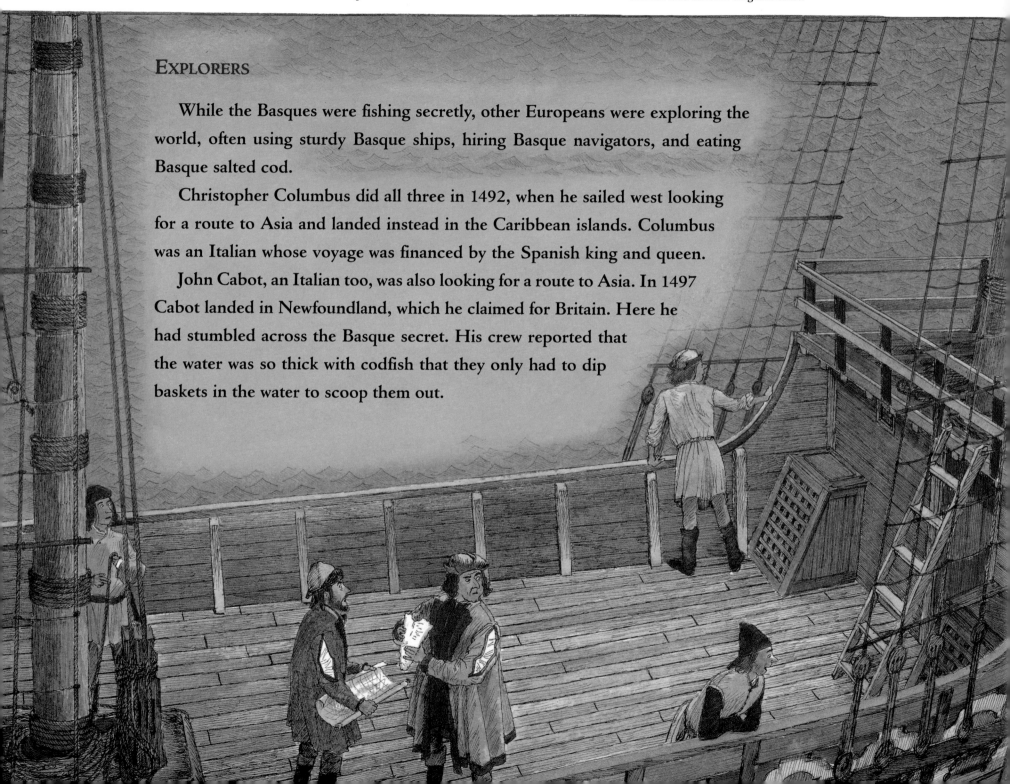

1492 Christopher Columbus sails to the Caribbean.

1497 John Cabot sails to Newfoundland, reports on the cod.

1524 Giovanni da Verrazzano finds and explores what is now New York Harbor and the New England coast.

EXPLORERS

While the Basques were fishing secretly, other Europeans were exploring the world, often using sturdy Basque ships, hiring Basque navigators, and eating Basque salted cod.

Christopher Columbus did all three in 1492, when he sailed west looking for a route to Asia and landed instead in the Caribbean islands. Columbus was an Italian whose voyage was financed by the Spanish king and queen.

John Cabot, an Italian too, was also looking for a route to Asia. In 1497 Cabot landed in Newfoundland, which he claimed for Britain. Here he had stumbled across the Basque secret. His crew reported that the water was so thick with codfish that they only had to dip baskets in the water to scoop them out.

1535 Jacques Cartier explores and claims the mouth of the St. Lawrence River for France. He spots 1,000 Basque fishermen in the area.

1576 Sir Martin Frobisher leaves England on the first of three voyages to find the Northwest Passage.

Soon everyone was coming to North America for the codfish. The Portuguese, the British, and the French all fished in the large cod schools off Canada. They reported seeing Basques. Some even said they heard local tribesmen speaking the strange Basque language. In the seventeenth century the rich cod fishing land was divided between the two most powerful nations, Britain and France. The Basques protested, saying that, as the discoverers, they too were entitled to a part of North America. All they wanted was the right to fish there. But they had never planted a flag, never made a claim, never told anyone, and now they had lost their fishing grounds.

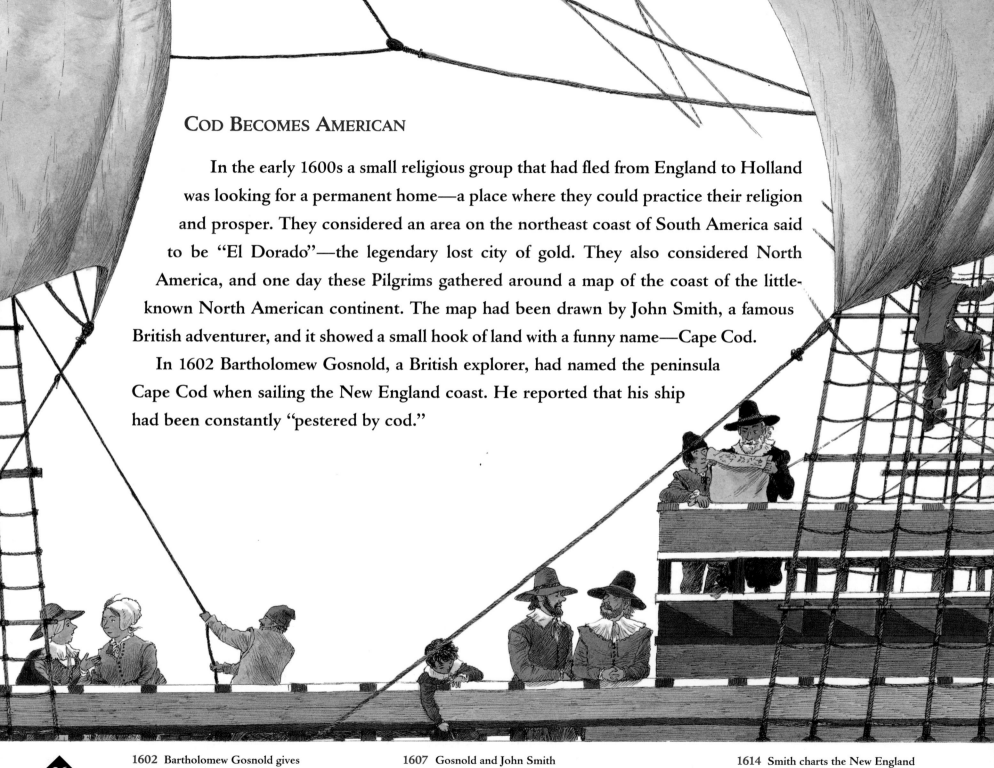

COD BECOMES AMERICAN

In the early 1600s a small religious group that had fled from England to Holland was looking for a permanent home—a place where they could practice their religion and prosper. They considered an area on the northeast coast of South America said to be "El Dorado"—the legendary lost city of gold. They also considered North America, and one day these Pilgrims gathered around a map of the coast of the little-known North American continent. The map had been drawn by John Smith, a famous British adventurer, and it showed a small hook of land with a funny name—Cape Cod.

In 1602 Bartholomew Gosnold, a British explorer, had named the peninsula Cape Cod when sailing the New England coast. He reported that his ship had been constantly "pestered by cod."

1602 Bartholomew Gosnold gives Cape Cod its name and reports on the wealth of cod in New England.

1607 Gosnold and John Smith help establish a permanent settlement in Jamestown, Virginia.

1614 Smith charts the New England coast and earns a fortune catching 47,000 cod and selling them in Spain.

In 1614 John Smith, who had helped establish a permanant British colony at Jamestown with Gosnold, charted the coastline of New England. He used Gosnold's name for the peninsula of Cape Cod. The voyage was famous for Smith having earned a fortune by catching 47,000 cod off the coast of America and selling them in southern Spain.

In 1620 the Pilgrims set sail on the *Mayflower* and landed near Cape Cod. Hoping to catch cod and sell it for great sums of money too, they decided to settle there and named their colony Plymouth.

1620 The Pilgrims land in Plymouth, Massachusetts.

TONGUES

"Tongues," which have a rich taste and gelatinous texture, are not really tongues, but the throat part under the chin.

STEWED CODFISH TONGUES

1 lb fresh codfish tongues
salt
1 large onion
pepper
½ lb clear pork fat

Place pork in fry pan and let cook until brown, add onion then tongues which have been cleaned well. Add salt and pepper to taste. Simmer about ½ hour.

—*From the Highlands and the Sea*, compiled by the Ingonish Women's Hospital Auxiliary, Ingonish, Cape Breton, Nova Scotia, 1974

WINTER IN MASSACHUSETTS

During their first two years in America, many Pilgrims starved to death. Winter in Massachusetts was snowy and so cold that some Europeans believed this new land was uninhabitable. The hungry Pilgrims could have survived on dried cod as the Vikings had done farther north, except the Pilgrims did not know how to fish or hunt. Nor did they know much about farming. Often they had to resort to stealing the hidden food reserves of the native people.

These natives called themselves Wampanoag. They made lines from vegetable fibers, made hooks from bones, and caught cod and other fish that swam near the coastline. They loved eating the clams they gathered on the shoreline and even showed the Pilgrims how to pry them open.

But the Pilgrims were not familiar with clams and would not eat them at first. Only in desperation, nearly starving, would they eat clams and lobster, which grew to great sizes and crawled out of the sea onto the beaches.

1623 The Pilgrims establish their first fishing station in Gloucester. It fails.

The Pilgrims were determined to succeed. They sent back to England for equipment and advice. They learned how to fish cod, dry it and salt it, and to plow the fish waste into the soil for fertilizer. From the Wampanoag they learned about farming local crops such as corn, beans, and squash. Slowly, as they became successful fishermen, they established fishing stations along the New England coast. Finally, they not only had food but something valuable to trade. In 1640 they sold a record 300,000 dried cod to Europe.

1625 They try again in Gloucester but fail again. They send to England for expert advice.

1640 The Massachusetts Bay Colony brings to market a record 300,000 cod.

THE COD REVOLUTION

By the 1650s, New England was becoming an important commercial center. Cod from the coast of New England, Labrador, Newfoundland, and Nova Scotia was brought to Boston and sold to merchants who shipped it to Europe. A city was being built around Boston's deep, sheltered harbor, and the waterfront was a forest of masts, cross spars, and rigging of ships from around the Atlantic.

One of Boston's leading trade partners was the Basque port of Bilbao. The Boston merchants sold cod to the Basques, and the Basques sold them oranges, wine, and products made of iron. More and more people moved to New England, not only to fish for cod, but to be merchants, shipbuilders, farmers, and craftsmen—carpenters, blacksmiths, barrel makers, furniture makers— to provide goods to a prosperous and growing colony. The cod trade transformed New England from a ragged pioneer outpost to a thriving society of growing cities and towns.

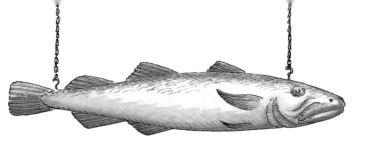

Cod became the symbol of prosperity. In Massachusetts, carvings of cod decorated houses, churches, and government buildings. The merchant families of Boston who grew wealthy trading cod became known as "the codfish aristocracy."

TO DRESS A CODS-HEAD, OR A FRESH COD

Take it and put it into a kettle, that hath a cover fitted to it, into which put 4 anchovies, six whitings, a quart of oysters with their liquor, a pint of shrimps, a pennyworth of Mace, two shellots, and after it hath simmered over the fire about an hour, take out the two jaw-bones, put in half a pound of sweet butter and serve it up. The like for a whole Cod, a Turbut, a Mullet.

—John Collins, *Salt and Fishery*, London, 1682

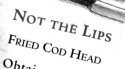

NOT THE LIPS
FRIED COD HEAD

Obtain 4 medium size cod heads. More for a large family. After they have been sculped (to sculp heads: with sharp knife cut head down through to the eyes, grip back of head firmly and pull) prepare to cook as follows: Cut heads in two, skin and remove lips. Wash well and dry. Dip both sides of head in flour, sprinkle with salt and pepper to taste. Fry in fat until Golden Brown on both sides. Serve with potatoes and green peas, or any other vegetable preferred.

—Mrs. Lloyd G. Hann, Wesleyville, Newfoundland
from *Fat-back & Molasses*, 1974

31

The Slave Trade

As early as 1645, Boston cod traders became involved in the great crime of their time—the slave trade. For years, Europeans had imported slaves from Africa and sent them to the plantations of the Caribbean.

Ships from New England sold high-quality salted cod to the Europeans, then they traveled to the Caribbean. There they sold the worst quality salted cod to Caribbean plantations to feed the thousands of Africans forced to work all day in the tropical sun, producing sugar. The Boston merchants would buy their molasses, which is made from sugar.

Back in New England the molasses was distilled into rum and sold in America and in Africa, where it was used to buy more slaves for the Caribbean—who would be fed the New England salt cod.

Accra

Codfish balls from the French Caribbean

1 kilo flour
1 packet powder yeast and a little baking
soda or it can be all baking soda.
Thyme, parsley, hot pepper, chive
(local green onion)
Soaked and flaked salt cod
Add one egg and beat together
Let rest one day
Spoon into hot oil.

—Carmelite Martial, *Le Table Creole*,
St. Felix, Guadeloupe

LABRADOR

NEWFOUNDLAND

BOSTON

NORTH
AMERICA

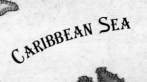

CARIBBEAN SEA

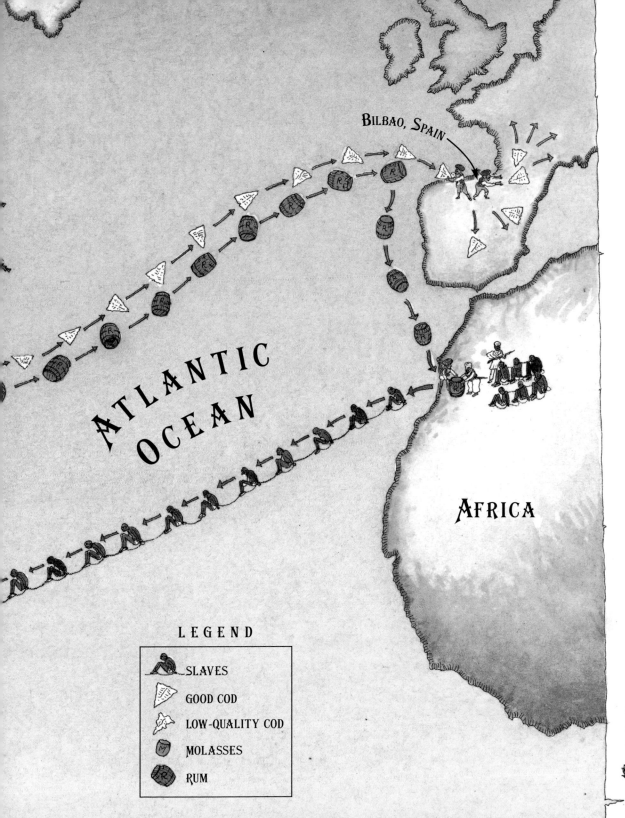

ATLANTIC OCEAN

BILBAO, SPAIN

AFRICA

LEGEND

In the American South, slaves modified African cooking for white people. After the Civil War, this process continued as many former slaves found jobs cooking for corporations or the railroad. "I was born in Murray County, Tennessee, in 1857, a slave. I was given the name of my master, D. J. Estes, who owned my mother's family, consisting of seven boys and two girls. I being the youngest of the family." So begins Rufus Estes' self-published book. Given the flaking technique in his recipe, the date, and place, the "codfish" is probably salt cod.

STEWED CODFISH

Take a piece of boiled cod, remove the skin and bones and pick into flakes. Put these in a stew pan with a little butter, salt and pepper, minced parsley and juice of a lemon. Put on the fire and when the contents of the pan are quite hot the fish is ready to serve.

—*Good Things to Eat*, Rufus Estes, 1911
"Formerly of the Pullman Company private car service and present chef of the subsidiary companies of the United States Steel Corporations in Chicago."

- 🧎 SLAVES
- △ GOOD COD
- ◁ LOW-QUALITY COD
- Ⓜ MOLASSES
- Ⓡ RUM

THE AMERICAN REVOLUTION

The New England colonies were ruled by the British government. When the British king decided to control the rebellious colonists by taxing them on important trade items such as molasses and tea, the colonists were furious. They had been doing well without British participation. Then further laws were passed that limited even the right of Americans to trade cod. But by then the American Revolution had begun.

From 1775 to 1781, thirteen of the American colonies fought the British. The colonies of the far north—Nova Scotia, Quebec, and Newfoundland—remained in the British Empire. It was too cold to fish for cod in their northern winters and so they did not develop as prosperous an economy as had given the lower thirteen a feeling of independence.

When, in 1782, they began to negotiate peace with the British, the most difficult point to resolve was the right of the newly independent Americans to fish cod.

1733 The British, trying to control the New England economy, declare a tax on molasses. It fails to slow trade.

1764 The British government tries again with the Sugar Act.

1765 The British further restrict Americans with the Stamp Act, followed by the Townshend Acts in 1767.

1773 Angry Americans dump tea into Boston Harbor.

Cape Cod kids don't use no sleds,
Haul away,
Heave away,
They slide down hills on codfish heads.

—Sea Shanty

In 1750, Captain Francis Goelet claimed that Marblehead, Massachusetts, was famous for its large, well-fed children who, he said, were "the biggest in North America." According to Goelet, "the chief cause is attributed to their feeding on cod's head which is their principal diet." But . . .

NOT THE EYES

FISHERMAN'S COD-HEAD CHOWDER

8 cod heads, the eyes removed	6 sliced potatoes
3 oz salt pork	butter
2 sliced onions	salt and pepper

Try out (render) the pork. Add the onions and fry until golden. Lay in a kettle, then add the cod heads and potatoes. Cover with cold water and cook till the potatoes are done. Season; add a good chunk of butter. Fishermen think removing the bones is sissy.

—*Vittles for the Captain: Cape Cod Sea-Food Recipes*
compiled by Harriet Adams, comments by N. M. Halper,
Provincetown, 1941

1775–1781
The American Revolution.

1781 The British surrender at Yorktown.

NOVEMBER 19, 1782 After years of arguing about cod fishing rights, a treaty is signed between the British and the new United States of America.

A New Kind of Revolution

The nineteenth century was a time of great change for Europe and North America. The skies of Britain, France, Germany, and the United States were blackening with the soot from factory chimneys. Engine power was replacing manpower. The British learned to produce steel inexpensively, and soon steel was replacing wood. New ships were made out of steel and driven by powerful engines.

1815 The French government equips its North American cod fishing fleet with longlines with more than a thousand hooks. Scientists begin worrying about overfishing.

1834 Slavery is abolished in the British Caribbean.

1848 Slavery is abolished in the French Caribbean.

At first, very little changed for fishermen. They still went to sea in wooden ships powered only by sails and lowered two-man rowboats in which to fish. The only modernization in the past few centuries had been that fishermen learned to bait a line a mile long with a thousand hooks instead of a short line with one or two.

Because the nineteenth century was an age of newfound sciences, scientists began asking: Are fishermen taking too many fish? If they had enough hooks, wouldn't they take all the fish in the ocean?

British scientists studied the ocean and the fish—both the herring that were used for bait and the cod they caught with it—and, by the 1880s, said that no matter how many fish fishermen took, there were so many fish in the ocean producing so many millions of eggs that the fishermen could go on taking as much as their boats would carry.

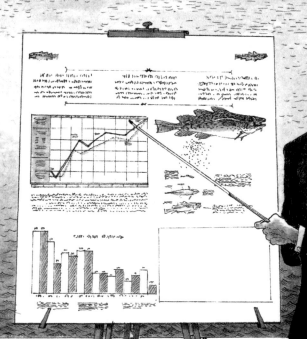

1862 A British commission led by Thomas Huxley concludes that overfishing with longlines is impossible.

1863 Slavery is abolished in the Dutch Caribbean. With the decline of sugar plantations, the New England–Caribbean cod trade almost disappears.

1881 The British build the first steam-powered cod fishing trawler, which drags a net over the side.

STEEL SHIPS

In the 1880s, the British invented a large, steel, engine-powered fishing boat that dragged a large net to catch fish. The British were catching and eating large amounts of cod. It was the base for the most popular British meal, fish and chips—batter-fried cod with french fries.

Soon all the nations of northern Europe fished with this type of boat. They all ate cod. The Danish ate it fresh with mustard for New Year's Eve. Sicilians ate salt cod for Christmas dinner. The Basques ate it salted with wonderful sauces. Caribbeans mashed their salt cod and ate it with hot peppers. The Portuguese fried it with potatoes.

The Europeans caught many more fish with their new steel ships. But after ten years there were fewer cod in northern Europe and the new ships were not catching as many. So they built even bigger ships with bigger nets and took more fish.

1892 The first otter trawl, the huge modern fishing net that drags chains on the bottom and has an enormous opening floating on the top, is built in Scotland.

1893 As an experiment, the U.S. government outfits a Cape Cod steam-powered fishing boat with an otter trawl.

FISH BALLS

A man went walking up and down
To find a place where he could dine in town.

He found himself an expensive place,
And entered in with modest face.

He took his purse his pocket hence,
But all he had was fifteen cents,

He looked the menu through and through,
To see what fifteen cents would do.

The cheapest item of them all
Was thirty cents for two fish balls.

The waiter, he, on him did call.
He softly whispered, 'one fish ball!'

The waiter bellowed down the hall,
'This creep here wants just one fish ball!'

The guests, they turned, both one and all,
To see who wanted one fish ball!

The man then said, quite ill at ease,
'And a piece of bread, Sir, if you please.'

The waiter bellowed down the hall,
'You get no bread with one fish ball!'

There is a moral to this all.
You get no bread with one fish ball.

Who would have bread with one fish ball,
Must get it first or not at all.

Who would fish balls with fixin's eat,
Must get some friend to stand the treat.

—Anonymous American

TWENTIETH CENTURY

In the early twentieth century, a young New Yorker named Clarence Birdseye went fur trapping in Labrador, Canada. He learned to freeze vegetables in the arctic wind, and could thaw them to feed his family during the long, cold winter. In 1924, he moved to the fishing port of Gloucester, Massachusetts, and established a frozen-fish factory. Now there was more than just salted cod and fresh cod. There was frozen cod.

Machines cut fillets and put them in boxes. Other machines cut fish into sticks. Frozen fish became a popular food for school lunches and in homes all over the United States, especially in places ocean fish had not been available before, such as the Midwest.

1921 A fish-filleting machine is developed in New England.

1924 New Yorker Clarence Birdseye develops the frozen-food process and establishes a frozen-fish plant.

Fishermen learned to freeze fish on their ships. Now they did not have to return to port to sell fresh fish. They could haul up thousands of tons of fish in giant nets, week after week, and keep them frozen. After World War II, submarine-hunting techniques such as spotter airplanes and sonar were used to find the fish in the ocean. The nets scraped along the bottom of the sea for miles.

There was no longer anyplace for a cod to hide.

1939–1945 World War II brings development of factory ships that can freeze fish on boats.

1950s Fish sticks become very popular.

41

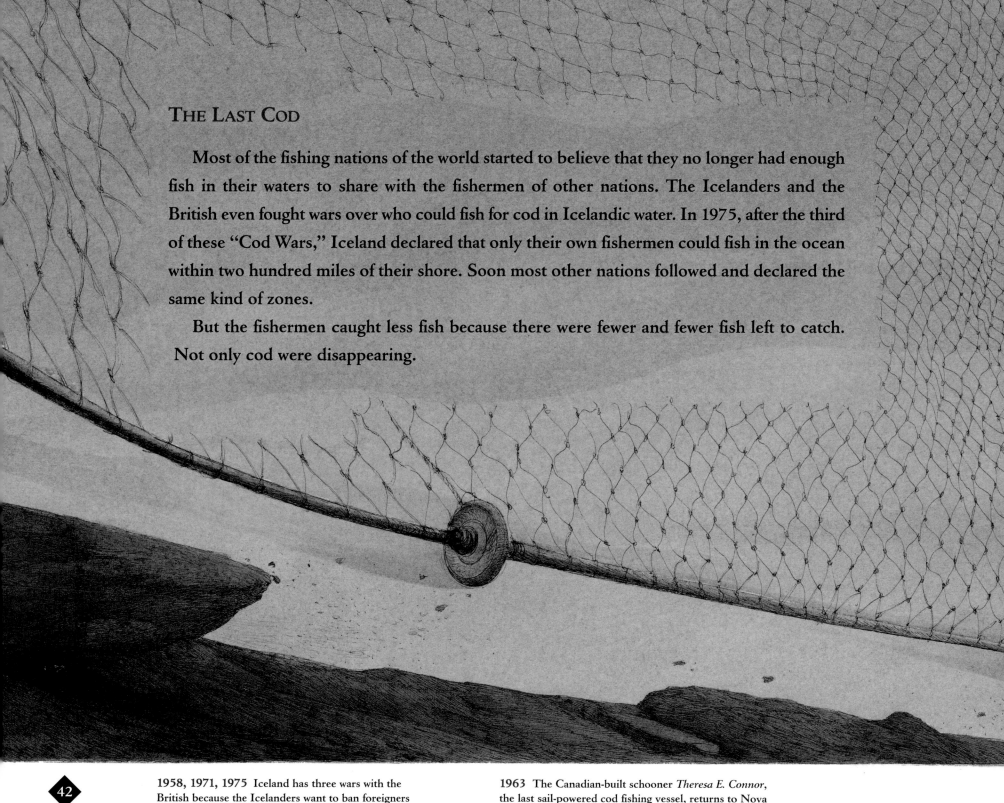

THE LAST COD

Most of the fishing nations of the world started to believe that they no longer had enough fish in their waters to share with the fishermen of other nations. The Icelanders and the British even fought wars over who could fish for cod in Icelandic water. In 1975, after the third of these "Cod Wars," Iceland declared that only their own fishermen could fish in the ocean within two hundred miles of their shore. Soon most other nations followed and declared the same kind of zones.

But the fishermen caught less fish because there were fewer and fewer fish left to catch. Not only cod were disappearing.

42

1958, 1971, 1975 Iceland has three wars with the British because the Icelanders want to ban foreigners from fishing for cod in Icelandic waters.

1963 The Canadian-built schooner *Theresa E. Connor*, the last sail-powered cod fishing vessel, returns to Nova Scotia, unable to find a crew to work her.

Now an estimated sixty percent of the species of fish that are popularly eaten are showing signs of disappearing. Tuna, swordfish, and salmon are becoming scarcer in the Atlantic. And with fewer fish in the Atlantic, fishermen are moving their big nets to the Pacific.

There are still a few cod left in the North Atlantic Ocean. But governments and fishermen have to learn how to limit what they catch or soon there will be no big fish left in the ocean at all. And then what will happen to the humpback whale, and the seals that eat cod bellies, and the birds that eat fish? And to the smaller fish that the cod eat? And to the smaller fish they eat? And to the zooplankton and the phytoplankton?

And what will happen to man if there are no more fish?

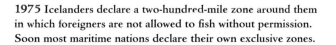

1975 Icelanders declare a two-hundred-mile zone around them in which foreigners are not allowed to fish without permission. Soon most maritime nations declare their own exclusive zones.

1992 The Canadian government, acknowledging that their cod population is near extinction, indefinitely bans cod fishing on the Grand Banks of Atlantic Canada, putting 30,000 fishermen out of work.

FOR FURTHER READING:

Baker, Lucy. *Life in the Oceans*. New York: F. Watts, 1990. 32 pages.

Bradford, William. *Homes in the Wilderness: A Pilgrim's Journal of Plymouth Plantation in 1620*. Edited by Margaret Wise Brown. Hamden, Conn.: Linnet Books, 1988. 76 pages.

Fritz, Jean. *Around the World in a Hundred Years: From Henry the Navigator to Magellan*. Illustrated by Anthony Bacon Venti. New York: G. P. Putnam's Sons, 1994. 128 pages.

Kipling, Rudyard. *Captains Courageous*. New York: The Century Company, 1896. 324 pages.

Kurlansky, Mark. *Cod: A Biography of the Fish That Changed the World*. New York: Walker Publishing Company, Inc., 1997. 294 pages.

Love, Ann, and Jane Drake. *Fishing*. America at Work Series. Illustrated by Pat Cupples. Toronto: Kids Can Press, 1999. 32 pages.

MacQuitty, Miranda. *Ocean*. Dorling Kindersley Eyewitness Books. Photographs by Frank Greenaway. New York: Dorling Kindersley, 2000. 64 pages.

Margeson, Susan M. *Viking*. Dorling Kindersley Eyewitness Books. Photographs by Peter Anderson. New York: Dorling Kindersley, 2000. 64 pages.

Martell, Hazel Mary. *Food & Feasts with the Vikings*. Parsippany, N.J.: New Discovery Books, 1995. 32 pages.

Matthews, Rupert. *Explorer*. Dorling Kindersley Eyewitness Books. Illustrated by Jim Stevenson. New York: Dorling Kindersley, 2000. 64 pages.

McClane, A. J. *The Encyclopedia of Fish Cookery*. Photographs by Arie deZanger. New York: Holt, Rinehart and Winston, 1977. 512 pages.

Parker, Steve. *Fish*. Dorling Kindersley Eyewitness Books. Photographs by Dave King and Colin Keates. New York: Dorling Kindersley, 2000. 64 pages.

Sewall, Marcia. *People of the Breaking Day*. New York: Atheneum, 1990. 48 pages.

Sewall, Marcia. *The Pilgrims of Plimoth*. New York: Atheneum, 1986. 48 pages.

Smith, C. Lavett. *National Audubon Society First Field Guide: Fishes*. New York: Scholastic Reference, 2000. 160 pages.

Vergoth, Karin, and Christopher Lampton. *Endangered Species*. Illustrated by George Stewart and Joe LeMonnier. New York: Franklin Watts, 1999. 112 pages.

Walker, Barbara. *The Little House Cookbook: Frontier Foods from Laura Ingalls Wilder's Classic Stories*. Illustrated by Garth Williams. New York: HarperCollins, 1979. 240 pages. (Includes a codfish balls recipe.)

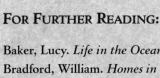

HUDSON BAY

LABRADOR

NEWFOUNDLAND

NORTH AMERICA

CAPE COD

ATLANTIC